An Emotional Journey

Jose Luis Figueroa

Order this book online at www.trafford.com
or email orders@trafford.com

Most Trafford titles are also available at major online book retailers.

Printed in the United States of America.

ISBN: 978-1-4907-5379-9 (sc)
       978-1-4907-5378-2 (e)

Library of Congress Control Number: 2015900441

Trafford rev. 01/13/2015

 www.trafford.com

North America & international
toll-free: 1 888 232 4444 (USA & Canada)
fax: 812 355 4082

Poetry Information

The poem titled **A Dead Man's Tale** found on page 20, is about a gentleman I met when I was in the hospital. He told me a little bit about his life and how it became fatal. After his story, he told me to pass it on and to never forget him. Two weeks went by until I wrote the poem, and it just happened to be the day he passed. I never knew his name, and so it's in the memory of the gentleman I like to call Mr. John Doe. Rest in peace.

Poems published or submitted in competitions are as follows:

<u>**Trouble**</u> was published in 1993 for ***Echos,*** a Passaic High School Pamphlet.

<u>**God is Love**</u> was published in 1993 for ***Echos,*** a Passaic High School Pamphlet.

<u>**Love**</u> was entered into competition in March 2002 and made the finals for the June 2002 competition, it was published in ***The Best Poems and Poets of 2002.***

<u>**My Thoughts of You**</u> was entered into competition in November 2001 and made the finals for the January 2002 competition, it was published in ***A Flood of Contentment in 2002.***

<u>**Feelings**</u> was entered into Poetry.com in June 2002.

<u>**What I Seek**</u> was entered into Poetry.com in June 2002.

<u>**A Realization**</u> was entered into Poetry.com in June 2002 and made semi finals.

Contents

The Early Years   **2**

Trouble—3
School—3
God is Love—4

Romance   **5**

Love —6
My Thoughts of You—6
Feelings —7
Emotions—7
You & Me—8
Thinking Back—8
Wishing You Near—9
The Way I Feel—10
Curious—11
Secret Love—12
Have to Let You Know—13
Guess Who?—13
Secret thoughts —14
Then Came You—14
Only If—15
Missing You—16
What I Seek —16

You—17
A Realization —17
Power of Love—18
You Got Me—18
True Love—19
Just Because—19
Friends—21
Relationships—21
Lonely—22
I Need Love—22
Why Me?—23
It Happens—23
Should It End?—24
A Dead Man's Tale—25
No One to Trust—26
You're Not the One—26
Wondering—27
Me & You? Ha!—27
Uncalled For—28
The Miracle of Birth—28
Thank You—29
Sorry—29
Trust—30
What Is...—30
How?—31

Strength—32
Challenges of Life—33
Questions—34
Going on—35
Choices—36
Starting Over—37
Life—37
Unpredictable Life—38
Mixed Emotions—38
It's Not Right—39
Meaning of Life—39
Heartbreaks—40
Insomnia—40
Sis—41
You See—42
Black Sheep—43
Rich—43
What's the Rush—44
Pain—44
My Journey—45
No One—46
Pain—47

Spanish   48

Amor—49
Dirme—49
Porque—50
Tu—50

Religious   51

Love from Above—52
Religion—52
Rain—53
Stressed—54
Am I Not Your Child—55
Depressed—56

Upcoming Poets   57

When—59
Prophet—60
Acknowledgments—61

The Early Years

Trouble

I go to the office,
I think I'm in trouble,
When all I did was blow a bubble,
"Where", they asked,
"Did you get the gum,"?
I had to answer, "From a bum,"
When I said that they replied,
"Bring the bum here!"
I asked, "Why?"
They said, "We want some gum."

School

Go to school,
That way you won't become a fool,
Some teachers are fun,
The people who don't listen always run,
Some students are nerds,
While the rest say, "School is for the birds,"
Some teachers are mean,
Others are afraid to be seen,
The Vice Principal drives anyone insane,
Always saying, "Use your brain."

God is Love

God is love,

He's as pure as a white dove,

Satan thinks he's smart,

But he forgets that we are a part,

Of Jesus Christ our savior,

God is divided in three,

The most powerful is he,

Jesus died on the cross for us,

He's the one to trust,

God gave us ten easy rules,

That way we won't act like fools,

His followers wrote the bible,

That talks about his title,

He came back from the dead,

The poor was fed,

He has a heart of gold,

That's why he wants to save our souls.

Romance

Love

Love was made for two,
It was made for me and you,
Love was made for us to share,
And to let others know how much we care,
Love was made for two special people,
Who will treat each other like they're equal,
True love never dies,
It just multiplies,
To have true love there must be trust,
Love just wouldn't be love without lust,
Love is made to cherish and respect,
If you don't have any of these; love is something you won't get.

My Thoughts of You

My thoughts of you are pure,
Of the night we spent together,
You're everything I want in a woman and more,
But you're so difficult to find,
Hoping the moment would last forever,
The thought of us meeting once again,
Lonely nights wishing you were near,
Praying we'll be more than just friends,
Awaiting the day to say, "I love you my dear,"
Those words which you said, that touched my heart,
Visions of us talking, laughing and holding hands,
Nothing on Earth could pull us apart,
Simply put, I want to be your man,
The person whom you'd love to kiss,
Your lips so soft and moist,
The warmth of your embrace, which is deeply missed,
Hopefully I'm the man of your choice.

Feelings

My feelings for you have gotten stronger,
I can't hold how I feel for you any longer,
When I'm with you I feel like everything could go our way,
My love for you will always stay,
It kills me just knowing it could've been us two,
And because of a simple mistake you're with someone new,
I hope these words won't scare you away,
It's just not easy to say,
Whenever we're together I can't resist kissing you passionately,
I will wait for you endlessly,
I love staring into your beautiful brown eyes,
I wish you were mine,
You're the only one I want to be with,
I was wrong to think love at first sight was a myth,
Hopefully you'll never disappear from my life,
I would like to have you as my wife.

Emotions

Love is like a fragile flower,
If treated right it will blossom and grow stronger,
True feelings come from the heart,
Feelings were made to express and show,
Few have the gift,
Others use it as a game to play with someone's emotions,
If you care for a loved one,
Let them know how you feel,
No matter how silly it may seem,
Or how difficult it may be,
Love starts off as something minor,
And builds up as time goes on.

You & Me

My feelings for you are extremely strong,
It's hard to believe we've been together this long,
A simple look or a cute smile is all it takes,
Your gentle touch, which makes me, shake,
The simple way you tease which turns me on,
When we're together we usually have fun,
Thoughts of our first night together,
The funny way you act so clever,
The cute name that you call me,
Always trying to find a way to get free,
Just to see me is so sweet,
While I find a way to sweep you off your feet,
The way I feel is hard to share,
I just want you to know I do care,
Remembering the first time we ever met,
Your kiss which I'll be waiting to get,
Hopefully we'll be together once again,
Soon we'll be in the park in the rain.

Thinking Back

From the moment I laid eyes on you,
I always wondered if there would ever be time just for you and me,
As time went on I tried to get you to realize I was alive,
Hoping someday you would be mine,
Never would have imagined you would've noticed me,
Until you called me around three,
The sound of your voice, which soothes my heart,
The depression I feel when we're apart,
No telling how long it would've taken me to let you know how I feel,
The first time we actually met I'll never forget,
The simple fact of me being with you made me content,
The great time we had that first night,
When we're together everything feels right.

Wishing You Near

Wondering when I will see,

You here with me,

Wishing you near is all I can do,

Until the time is right when it is just us two,

When I see you it brings me joy, and a smile to my face,

Every time I'm with you my heart pounds, as if I were in a race,

I've never met anyone as unique as you,

This is one of the many reasons why my heart is true,

Even when you're not near I can still hear your sweet voice,

I'm still shocked that you picked me as your choice,

Hard to believe a simple phone call made a difference,

You and I were meant to be together,

Don't let anyone lead you to believe, that I just want you for one thing now or ever,

I hope you do realize everything I say; do, or act is from the heart,

Wishing you near is what I do every night we're apart,

I just want you to know I'll never do you wrong,

If I had a singer's voice I would sing you a romantic song,

If I were a millionaire I would buy you the biggest diamond ever found,

If everything goes as well as I intend; you will always have me around,

These are a few examples to express how strong my feelings are for you,

Then again you probably didn't have a clue,

So until I see you once again,

I'll lie in my bed before ten,

Wishing you near,

Waiting for you to lie next to me, my dear.

The Way I Feel

Sometimes I have feelings I can't explain,
Why when I'm alone I feel so much pain,
Together I feel whole,
Apart I feel shallow and cold,
No one makes me feel special the way you do,
Some may say I'm a fool to spend even a few minutes with you,
But I don't care what they say,
Because that's why their relationships never stay,
Day or night you're always on my mind,
For two people to click like we did is hard to find,
All I ask is for a little bit of your time,
To help you relax and unwind,
So here's a kiss from me to you until we meet,
Until we're together sharing each other's heat.

Curious

I want to get to know you better,
It's hard to find someone who's funny, cute, and clever,
I would like to be more than just friends,
If that were to happen I'd be thankful to the end,
I meant to ask you if you had a man,
Just to find where I might stand,
This is the only way I can ask you,
Cause I don't want to feel like a fool,
With a possibility of saying something that might sound stupid or
making it sound like something it's not,
Just want you to know I think you're hot,
Hoping your answer is anything instead of no,
Praying we have a good time while we bowl,
If anything were to start between us I'll never do you wrong,
Even though we won't be together on Thursday real long,
I'll cherish every moment spent,
Everything I wrote I meant,
Please let me know what you think and to see,
If you would like to go out with me,
If you do I would like to take it nice and slow.

Secret Love

The feelings I have is so profound,
Never thought I would feel like this for someone that just came to town,
How I feel I guess you'll never know,
Always wondering how far we could go,
Looking for love is never easy,
It may seem that what you search will never be,
You may not think of me but I think of you,
Thinking when I should give you a clue,
Afraid of being hurt,
Hoping you won't treat me like dirt,
From the first glance I admired your beauty,
To get with you would be my duty,
I know I would treat you right,
Trying to figure out what night,
To tell you all I think of is only you in my life.

Have to Let You Know

I see you almost everyday,
Usually not knowing what to say,
I know you just want to be friends,
Just want you to know I'm not like all men,
There is more to me than what others see,
When you need someone to trust; trust in me,
I know what I wish will never come true,
One day being more that just friends; me and you,
I just hope things aren't as bad as they seem,
Wishing it'll be just like in my dreams.

Guess Who?

If you only knew how I feel about you; you wouldn't believe it,
And if you only knew how I would love to make you happy,
You wouldn't even begin to imagine who I could be,
I know you don't think of me as much as I think of you,
Just to give you a clue, I'll give you two descriptions,
I'm pure Puerto Rican and I have eyes that change color,
Your wish is for someone who'll love you and your child,
Who will also be faithful and caring about your feelings,
I like being around you simply because of your unique personality,
You're funny, fine, and never needs to bulls----,
Always letting people know what's on your mind,
Not caring who it may be friend, family, etc,
By now you might have an idea,
If you do ask the person,
I chose to write rather that tell you in person just in case you weren't
interested that way I won't feel dumb,
Also you're always going somewhere when I'm near,
That's enough hints.

Secret thoughts

I've been thinking about you for quite some time,
Hoping one day that you would be mine,
Whenever I'm near you, I've been dying to tell you how I feel,
To assure you if we ever got together, my love would be real,
Knowing you won't be hurt ever again,
Dreaming we'll be more than friends,
Just thinking of the beautiful smile you have,
The things you do to make me laugh,
I enjoy being around you,
Damn if you only knew,
How great we would be together,
Then our lives would be much better.

Then Came You

I've been looking for love in all the wrong places,
Looking for the special one in a crowd of faces,
Then I saw you,
Being next to you knowing you would make my gray skies blue,
You are all I think of morning, noon, and night,
I would like to get to know you better,
Now or whenever,
You make my life worth living,
My love is what I'm offering,
A part of my heart is what you've taken.

Only If

I've only known you for a short period of time,
Wondering if you would give me a chance to be with you,
Knowing you're so fine,
Thoughts of the two of us together seems to good to be true,
There's probably no chance I'll be part of you're life,
Knowing this tears my heart like a knife,
The way I feel for you; words can't begin to explain,
Hoping you would feel the same,
Thinking how I'll let you know,
And let my feeling show,
Right now all I can do is admire you from a distance,
Not looking to anxious or persistent,
Wishing you would be here next to me,
Even though I know my luck will never change as I can see.

Missing You

I am in need of your warm embrace,
I miss the way your skin feels,
To touch your silky soft flesh,
To kiss your luscious, soft, moist lips,
To experience the feelings which is so hard to explain,
Love,
Holding your body close to mine,
To caress those areas on your body which needs my touch,
Just anticipating what part of your body to fondle next,
To kiss those spots which make you quiver,
To cuddle and wrap you in my arms,
Hoping I give you the sense of security which you might yearn,
Knowing the love we'll share,
Is too strong to diminish.

What I Seek

Beauty is not only skin deep,
Beauty from within is what I seek,
Someone who's eyes glisten in the moonlight,
Someone who makes my heart beat quicker when she's in my sight,
I seek someone who's not afraid to show how she feels,
Imagining there is someone out there that will love me for real,
A person who's funny and smart,
Allowing me to show what's in my heart,
And all these things I have found in you,
You have taught my heart love, that's true,
When I'm angry you lighten up my day,
When you're around there's never a dull moment,
Tu amor siempre esta en mi corazón,
Hoy, mañana, y para siempre,
Y esta es la razón porque yo nunca te dejare,
Sabiendo que tu eres la única para mi,
Yo soy el único que te va acer feliz.

You

You are the flame that never dies out,
You are my hope,
When all my sadness consumes me,
You are my heart,
The one who I will always worry and care for when you let me,
You are my sanity,
At a time when I am lost without love,
Yes,
You are the one who makes my life worth living.

A Realization

You are my shining star in the dark blue sky,
You are my hope in a world of chaos,
You have faith in me when no one else gave me a chance,
You gave me love when I began to lose hope,
You taught me that I am someone special,
You are the one who let me know that I was not alone in losing faith in
finding true love,
These are a few reasons how you have changed my life and how I know
you're the perfect one for me,
This world was heartless and cold,
With no one to hold,
Then…
God sent down an angel just for me,
To marry and cherish,
And to know how true happiness should really be,
A person to care for and love,
Simply because she is my gift from above.

Power of Love

Through all the times we struggled together,
In the best of times and the worst of times,
No matter what the situation was, we overcame it together,
Loving each other even though we knew each others' imperfections,
Showing everyone that our love has no boundaries,
Not caring what lonely and depressed individuals say about us in a jealous rage,
Always having our love helps us conquer hurdles and bumps while still staying strong,
Although many people said our love would not last,
And once again our love proved to be stronger than anyone hoped for or expected,
No one shall break this bond,
Only the two in love can break it,
And if it's up to our hearts; this love of ours will never die,
Philosophers say only time can tell,
But in the matters of the heart only the couple in love are allowed to say,
Keeping the love strong and erotic maybe a difficult task,
If the couple with a bond so strong,
This part of life is no more challenging than living, eating, or breathing,
Every love including ours will have its' ups and downs,
This is when the test of true love will challenge the unsuspecting couple,
If the love is true; it will protect the two united from any heartache,
Believing in each other is what we're going to do,
So our love can be remembered as on of the greatest loves ever known.

You Got Me

You got my mind, body, and heart,
I quiver with the sound of your voice,
Images of us together for a brief moment in time,
Discussing all my love can offer you,
Honesty, loyalty, romance, and sensuality,
Everything you deserve and more,
Give my love a chance and you'll see,
The one you seek is me.

True Love

True love has a way of finding its match,
We never know when or who or how far away,
But it finds it anyhow,
You know when it's true love when you're happy,
And that special someone is almost everything you need and want,
The attraction whether through words or sight happens almost instantaneously,
Searching for true love is a lost cause,
It'll find you when you least expect it,
So make sure once it's found you; you never let it go,
Because it might not find you ever again.

Just Because

I know I don't always show how much I appreciate you and all you do,
Sometimes I may not tell you how beautiful you look,
I also know I'm a pain in the neck, hard headed, and you want to choke
the life out of me at times,
But no matter what… I love you,
I do appreciate everything you've done and are still doing,
If I could pay you back for all the wonderful things you've ever done,
said, or even shown,
I would never be able to,
Sometimes I forget that your self-esteem isn't what it used to be,
You constantly put yourself down and say you're ugly,
When on the contrary you're beautiful,
Your smile makes people around you get in a better mood,
You'll never know what your happiness means to me,
This is why I try to d things to shock you and make you forget about
whatever it is that's troubling you at the moment,
My mission in life is to take care of the family,
Family- meaning making you happy whether you need it or not,
Here is a small token of appreciation and something beautiful for a beautiful person,
You,
The one I love.

Life

Friends

Many don't know what it means to be a friend,
Those who do know it means to be true to the end,
No need for lies and deception,
A true friend would be understanding in any situation,
True friends are there when you need them,
Not fighting over women or men,
Or just use them for their money,
Instead hook them up with a cute honey,
Let them know you can be trusted,
Even if they look busted,
Just be there for advice,
Or to lend them a device,
When you're stressing they know just what to say,
Letting you know it'll be O.K.

Relationships

Trying to find a match is hard,
It doesn't hurt to show how you feel with a simple card,
If you find that special person treat them right,
Try to resolve your problems without a fight,
Always keep the love alive,
Or else they'll find someone who has a better sex drive,
Love is not all about sex,
It's about showing you're not like the rest,
When you're married it should change for better not worst,
If it changes for the worst you'll swear the idea was a curse,
The feeling for you love one should be like the day you met,
If you don't give your love one attention love you won't get.

Lonely

Here alone with no one to care for,
Don't know if I want to search anymore,
It's hard to find love,
As pure as a white dove,
I don't want to spend the rest of my life alone,
I would rather spend it talking to someone special on the phone,
Life is such a cruel place since I have no one to share my love with.

I Need Love

I need someone to care for,
Someone who doesn't care that I'm poor,
I've never been lucky to find my one & only,
Knowing this makes me feel very lonely,
A caring person to give my love to,
The true love I've been searching for from the day I was born 'till the age
of twenty-two,
It's hard to describe how I feel,
From all the heartache and pain my heart is as cold as steel,
All I can do is pray to find someone who'll bring me joy.

Why Me?

I met a woman, who was one of a kind,
I thought maybe she could be mine,
In time I began to realize it could never be,
If she wasn't faithful to her husband she won't be to me,
So I guess the best thing she did was let me go,
Know the answer to her loving me was no,
Now I know she didn't give a damn,
Simply because she had another man,
I tried to show & give her a good time,
But she was always looking for the next person in line,
At times I wished to be with her once again,
Even though I know she's not worth it.

It Happens

Sometimes the person you love may not love you,
It may be painful but true,
Some use you just for sex,
Few get with you because of the way you looked when you flex,
Not everyone was cut out for romance,
Others don't allow anyone in their heart and take a chance,
Of being hurt once again,
Knowing your friends were right all along,
Saying she's all wrong for you,
Making sure you don't get hurt as she goes out the door,
Your heart will feel pain but it won't last,
Soon enough you'll find someone who'll make you forget about the past,
Many look for love in all the wrong places,
Making your life feel like you're going through mazes.

Should It End?

Life can be so depressing sometimes you wish it would just end,
Not listening to good advice from a friend,
Have to make sure that your life doesn't get that bad,
Wishing to die without being a dad,
Have to remember life isn't as bad as it seems,
Just try to live a dream,
No matter how silly or daring,
As long as you try it with someone who's caring,
It you end it today you'll never know what tomorrow will bring,
If you end it you'll never get you heavenly wings,
Tomorrow maybe worst or it maybe better,
It really doesn't matter,
As long as your time as clever as you possibly can,
Just remember you're only human,
You're not the only one who's made mistakes,
If you ever feel like ending it take a break,
And realize the ones who care for you and how they'll feel,
Also for family members who kneel,
Before God for your well being.

A Dead Man's Tale

I met a female fine as can be,
I knew she would get with me,
Once we were together life was good,
Then I met her sister, who just moved in the hood,
Soon enough I was seeing both at the same time,
Neither one suspecting they both were mine,
Now my life seemed to be better,
Swore I was the man for being so clever,
Got intimate with both and got bored,
So I got a cheap whore to do the things the others wouldn't do,
Thinking now this was the life one on the side plus two,
Not knowing the whore had HIV,
This lasted for at least three months until everyone began to notice a change in me,
Both sisters got pregnant and gave birth,
One died because of the virus; the other survived with the baby but
wanted nothing to do with me,
Now knowing I have AIDS my life ain't worth S___,
Hoping others learn from my mistakes,
To think I could've prevented this with a simple rubber,
For anyone who thinks of having sex remember me,
And think; is your partner clean enough to do without protection?

No One to Trust

No one to trust who do you turn to,

People whom you thought were your friends acting as if they don't know you,

No one around who understands your pain,

Trying to be normal in a world that's insane,

Afraid of being an outcast among everyone else,

Who should I trust where could I go,

When the closest person to you is your foe,

The hope to find someone who knows what I'm going through,

Living my life without a clue,

My only friend a chrome-plated gun,

Never knowing what it was to have fun,

Life in the ghetto is never what it seems,

All I ever knew was how to make cream,

If you ever need a hand I'll be around,

Don't ever trust anyone you just found.

You're Not the One

I don't have the heart to tell you,

I found someone new,

The feelings I once had for you are gone,

Finding a way to tell you was hard and long,

How it happened I don't know it just did,

I'm sorry to say it kid,

What we had would never last,

Have to agree we did have fun but that's the past,

Just hope you won't hate me forever,

It's just that I've found someone better,

I hope we can still be friends,

Soon you'll find someone to mend your broken heart,

Now that we're apart,

Just want to let you know I do still care,

And you won't find anyone who'll treat you as well as I did anywhere.

Wondering

Alone and unaware what lies ahead,
Wondering and sometimes wishing I were dead,
No one to hold and cherish,
Hoping my one wish comes true,
Waiting until someone finds out how I feel or gets a clue,
Anticipating that someone special fills the void of happiness,
Any chance of love seems hopeless,
But I still manage to search and struggle,
To find the right one to hold and cuddle,
Many times before I thought I had love and affection,
Instead I was involved in lies and deception,
Praying to find someone that won't hurt me just like the others in the past,
Wishing that the next relationship would last.

Me & You? Ha!

For those who broke my heart,
Still wondering why we're apart,
Thought you could play me for a fool,
Treated me like a mule,
Hoping I wouldn't let go,
Asking if there's any chance of being together once again I'll say NO,
Think I'll want you back after all you did,
Just remember I'm not a kid,
No one should be hurt the way you hurt me,
Any fool can see,
What you wanted was not to be with me long term,
For what you did at the time I was hoping you would rot and burn,
We were great together,
Luckily now I'm doing better,
With or without you I will survive,
For there is someone out there who will make me feel alive.

Uncalled For

A child doesn't deserve to feel pain and torture,
To die just because you couldn't take the responsibility,
Or because you didn't know how to say no,
The pain isn't only felt by the mother but by the father,
If not consulted by the father; he may feel the pain somewhat harder than the mother,
Thoughts or hopes of having a child left unknown,
The plans of how you would care for the child now only leaving an enormous void,
Asking why it was done without you knowledge,
Knowing you were completely against it from the very beginning,
Abortion is understandable for certain circumstances,
Not for foolish or selfish reasons,
Only wanting to hold your child at birth,
Now having nothing but pain and depression,
The hope of loving your child torn from your heart,
Respect and trust for you companion lost.

The Miracle of Birth

Hard to believe what the power of love can make,
A baby whose life is in your hands,
To care for and teach,
Show the good and the bad,
And let them know you'll always be there,
No matter what the circumstances,
They'll rely on you to make the right calls,
Even if you don't know what exactly to do,
As parents we are their shield in a time of crisis,
We are also their friend when they need someone
to talk to.

Thank You

Thank you for being there when I was sick,

Thank you for understanding me when no one else did,

Thank you for disciplining me when I need to be,

Thank you for standing by my side even though you knew it wasn't the right choice,

Thank you for letting me learn from my mistakes,

Thank you for being there when I made the wrong decision while you were hoping it would go well; even though you didn't approve,

Thank you for being my back bone when I needed someone to lean on,

Thank you for being my best friend whom I could confide in,

And finally I thank you for taking the responsibility of raising me unlike many who just leave their kids out in the streets,

Thank you for being the mom others' wished was theirs to begin with,

I love you,

Sorry for all the trouble I have caused up to this very day,

Your job was not easy and you got no sick day for,

But you still did it because you are my mom.

Sorry

Please forgive me for not being the son you wanted me to be,

Now that I am older I know you were tough with me so I would become a good man,

Maybe I never showed it but you are my idol,

The man who won the battle of alcoholism,

I'm sorry for making life stressful for you and mom,

Your wisdom maybe unusual but I still appreciate it,

I wish we had a father-son bond a long time ago,

You were always there for me when I got in trouble,

Hope you remember I may not be as wise or experienced in life,

But if you want to vent or talk I'm here just in case,

No matter what,

I love you dad,

Hopefully by now you already know.

Trust

Trust is a bond that is earned not given,
This bond is easy to break but hard to get,
To some it may take years to earn,
For others it may take a few days,
Trust consist of honesty, loyalty, and respect,
This is not easy to do for many,
Once the bond is broken the relationship will never be the same,
That's when confusion and doubt sets in,
And to get the trust of the individual back will be virtually impossible,
Lies and deception could be one of the biggest reasons why many relationships end,
Due to lack of trust,
Every relationship whether it is friendship, matters of the heart, or it's
having to deal with family members all need it,
Without it; life itself becomes difficult,
Making it unbearable to enjoy life and all it has to offer,
Trust is needed for everything we do,
In a work environment; responsibility is another form of trust,
If you are not responsible enough to complete a task you will not be trusted.

What Is...

What is a man without a heart,
What is a heart with no love,
What is love with no one to share it with,
What is a special someone when they can't be found,
What is a man with a heart and love to give; all alone,
Dead, cold, depressed, frustrated, and lonely,
What,
You thought you were the only one feeling like this?
Look around you,
Why do you think we have a lot of angry, bitter people in this world?
For all these exact reasons.

How?

How can I feel proud,

Knowing no matter how hard I try,

I can never manage to do anything right,

How can I feel stress free,

When the only way I can make my family happy is by showing them how much I love them,

How can I feel like a real man,

When I feel like I am not a great lover, husband, father, or provider,

How can I tell my wife everything is all right,

When I feel the world around me is crumbling down,

Bills keep piling up,

And of course,

My daughters and wife; whom I love with all my heart,

I would love to buy them clothes and other trickets but I have no money to spend,

How can I do all this and not lose my sanity nor my loved ones,

The only way I know how,

By hoping and praying that the love my wife & I have will help guide us though those rough times,

Even when it seems humanly impossible,

We'll stand strong and handle it together,

The best way we can,

So we can live happily together,

Because this is all we will ever need for as long as God permits us to.

Strength

This family has been through a lot,
Their smiles hide all scars life has given them,
Using their God given strength,
They go through life battling handicaps and illnesses,
But by looking at them you would never know,
The son's character is way beyond his years,
Trying to keep strong for his mother and sister,
The daughter is so smart and so caring,
Trying to let everyone know it's going to be alright,
The mother has a will so strong that it would move mountains,
Letting her children know she will always be there for them,
To know this family is to love them,
This family is an inspiration to us all,
No matter what the situation is; keep going,
Never letting anything or anyone stand in your way,
Fighting and surviving the world's most difficult game,

Challenges of Life

In life many challenges may come your way,

In death all that could've been accomplished never will,

Yesterday is still so close,

Today just won't go away,

Tomorrow seems like it'll never arrive,

My first name is stress,

My middle name is pain,

I still don't have a last name because my problems barely ever seem to get resolved,

I give my all but it's never enough,

I try to get away from all whom or what might make me lose my sanity,

During the challenges; it seems like I'll never see a better day,

During the night everything I got away from somehow followed me,

When the better day gets here I pray that it doesn't end,

It feels like no one knows my anguish or what I'm going through,

All I'll need is that one person; to motivate me by giving a word of advice or a word of comfort,

To reassure me that in time,

Eventually, everything will turn out just fine.

Questions

Why is it that the only luck I have is bad luck,

Why do I help everyone out; just to have those same people turn around and betray me,

Why do I try so hard; but only get so far,

Why; when I try something new, all I get is a negative response,

Who is to say how my life should be; if I don't know where I'm going to end up,

All I can do is take my life day by day,

Deal with everything as it comes,

When advised; I'll take the positive and reject the negative,

No one can tell me how to live my life or take care of my family,

Expect the worst and hope for the best,

This is the quote I live by,

I'll continue to assist those who seem to need it,

And expect nothing in return except for honesty, respect, and friendship,

Until that day comes that I have overcome all odds stacked against me,

Proving that I make my own fate and no one else can derive me from my
own goals and accomplishments.

Going on

I once heard a saying, "Failure is not when you fall, failure is when you
fall and choose not to get up",
I have made many mistakes in my life,
I probably will make more in the future,
Most of those errors were from making the wrong choices,
Sometimes I just felt like giving up,
But luckily for my family I didn't,
Because of them; they are the reason why I still live and breathe,
Everyone has their own motivation, philosophy, or reason why they are where they are,
Mine is boiled down in one word "Family",
My daughters and my wife need me to be level headed,
Become a positive roll model for my daughters,
And somehow make any or all problems vanish,
Even if I have no idea how to do it,
For my family; just for the sake of my loved ones,
Because they are my reason for going on.

Choices

So many decisions to make in a short period of time,

How will I know if I chose the right one,

When I don't have any time to make any mistakes,

I don't want my family to be disappointed in me,

Wondering if they should've let me go because of all the wrong choices I have made,

I know they are suffering,

I hate seeing them like this,

All the pressure rests on my shoulders,

I feel like I can't go on,

But failure is not an option for me,

The day I'll stop trying is when I'm dead and buried,

I never would've imagined it would be like this,

But no matter how I feel; I'll still keep fighting,

To correct the wrong that were done,

And keep finding the right choices to keep my family whole,

So they know; it was a good thing that they stayed with me no matter what.

Starting Over

Starting over is never easy,
All old habits and acquaintances must be left behind,
The past should stay in the past,
Sometimes life gets so tough that you feel like going back to the old way of life,
The key to leaving the past is changing the lifestyle completely,
Doing what was easy to do before will only bring all old problems back,
Sometimes making a new beginning; saves a man's sanity or pride for life itself,
It's easier said than done; but it's possible,
In the long run; you will see,
Everything you work so hard to build,
Will have all the negative or jealous people regretting that they should've
backed you up when times were tough,
The only thing needed is will power to help guide you,
This is the only way you'll achieve your goal,
Which is starting over or starting a new life,
Legally without worrying about hurting any loved ones,
Who so desperately pray that you'll change your ways.

Life

Life is too short to screw up,
Too long to be locked up,
Enjoy it to the fullest,
Live to enjoy the simple pleasures of life; parties, romances, and children,
Choose all decisions wisely,
Certain choices can help you become very successful or miserable,
Every choice reflects on how your family and peers will perceive you,
Thinking before reacting will prolong and protect your life,
Acting recklessly can get you incarcerated or maybe into an early grave,
Cherish life; so when your old and gray,
You'll have stories to tell your children and their children about,
While lecturing our next generation on how to live and enjoy life,
And always try to avert any dangerous situations which could endanger
you or your loved one.

Unpredictable Life

Life is an interesting thing,
One minute you're in a great relationship,
The next minute you're looking for someone else who'll make you happy,
New relationships are nerve wrecking,
Hoping your new love won't hurt you like the previous one,
Life is always unpredictable,
It sends love to you; but you never know if it's the right one for you,
Only time will tell if that love is truly the "one" you've seeked.

Mixed Emotions

How could I love you if you don't love me,
I found someone who'd be able to love me the way I need to be loved,
Now what do I do when I love you and I could be with another who would love me more,
I'm torn between the one I love and the one who is willing to love me,
Lord,
Please help me make the right decision,
Cause right now I don't know what to do.

It's Not Right

How could you be so kind hearted but so naïve,

No man has the right to hit a woman,

After all you've done for him; he repays you with a smack,

You need someone who'll appreciate you for who you are,

Leave him before it's too late,

His next hit could be your last,

It's not right that he treats his mistress better than you,

Be strong and do what you must,

He's not worthy of your love,

Cause if you don't the only love you'll get is everyone's last respects.

Meaning of Life

What is the meaning of life?

This is a question that no one can honestly answer,

This is what life means to me,

Enjoying the time spent with you children,

Letting your loved ones know how you feel,

Living, loving everyday one another as if it were your last day,

Because you never know when it is,

Happiness, excitement, ecstasy,

All part of what life should be,

And if it's not then you're not enjoying what life has to offer.

Heartbreaks

You're heartbroken,

Who do you turn to when your friend/ lover/ companion is the cause of it?

Everyone gives you advice but, you're not ready to listen,

Waiting for a sign that this was a horrible nightmare,

When you awake you're still heartbroken and nothing was resolved,

Should the relationship end or give it another shot,

If you give it another try good just remember give it your all and don't forget the past,

If you move on give yourself time to recover and your heart a chance for happiness,

The pain is temporary,

You deserve better never settle,

The right one for you will appear,

All it'll take is time.

Insomnia

I can't sleep,

Thoughts of how my loved one doesn't love me,

I tried to be the best man I could,

And she still wants another,

I work for the family,

I try to be a good father, husband, and still my best isn't enough,

How can I sleep knowing that the one who lies next to me,

Won't be around 'till death do us part,

My kids will be heartbroken,

My heart will be hollow once again,

If and when I move on why should I love again,

If all I have to look forward to is heartache,

Do you see why I can't have a goodnight's rest.

Sis

Why don't you just obey mom,

She does everything for you,

Instead; all you do is cause her grief,

Can't you see you're hurting her,

I don't appreciate how you disrespect her,

Please change your ways if not for me at least for her,

Everytime she's proud of you and tries to show it,

You do something to disappoint her,

I love you,

I hope you know that,

But I beg of you; please open your eyes and see,

The you treat her just can't be,

If you're stressed out and you feel you can't talk to mom or dad remember,

Call me,

I'll always be here for you even though I don't show it,

You're my baby sister and I'll always love you.

You See

Now you're scared you'll lose me forever,

If you weren't looking for new love this wouldn't have happened,

You ignored my love,

I've been there when everyone turned their back on you,

I've been your backbone and you've been mine,

Then you lost the love for me for another,

Just when you thought it was over you finally realized,

That what you were looking for was right in front of you all along,

The one who'll love you unconditionally,

If you do what you have to do and love me the way I need to be loved you'll have nothing to fear,

Just remember if you won't love me,

Someone else will love me the way I'm suppose to be loved,

It's not a threat; it's the truth,

I love you,

Don't forget we're together out of love,

I don't need anyone else but you,

Give my love an opportunity to prove to you that it'll be here for you if you truly want me,

If you do then I'll be here 'till death do us part.

Black Sheep

Everyone complains that being the black sheep of the family is the worst,
I tend to disagree,
Don't tell me you don't like the feeling of proving everyone wrong,
Being the black sheep is like being the underdog of life,
Someone always has something negative to say about us,
Then, when we accomplish what they said even they couldn't do they're astonished,
Don't look this as a negative in your life,
The bright side is when everyone expects you to fail,
Rise above the negativity and prove to them that what they said has no impact on your life,
Don't let anyone stand in the way of your dreams, hopes, or ambitions,
You're in charge of your own destiny.

Rich

What is it to truly be rich,
You could have a lot of money and still not be rich,
Being rich is…,
Being alive everyday and enjoying what life has to offer,
Having the privilege of watching your children grow up and seeing, hearing, all of their "firsts",
The feeling you get when you do good for a family member or a loved one or just a good deed,
The ability to spend time with your family and splurging when you're with them,
Feeling loved and giving love right back,
Money, jewelry, fancy clothes, and cars are all materialistic,
True wealth can never be replaced or mourned,
Don't make jokes about those that don't have the things you do,
You never know if these same people already have all they'll ever need or want.

What's the Rush

What's going on with the young girls now a days,

They haven't gotten to high school yet and already they want to bare children,

They should enjoy their youth before trying to raise one,

Fine she might be great with kids but these kids always go home,

When she has her own there will not be anyone picking that child up when the baby begins to misbehave,

And some other young girls want to leave home,

Certain circumstances are understandable,

For instance; mental, physical, or emotional abuse,

But wanting to be out because their parent told them that they weren't allowed to go out with their friends,

Or because they asked the parents for something and was denied,

Even if the parents are getting on their nerves because they aren't able to get everything their way,

Remember,

The parents' job is to make sure nothing bad happens to you,

Please young ladies of tomorrow be patient,

You might miss something special if you rush.

Pain

My heart feels like it's ripping apart,

You said you love me but you're not in love with me,

Are you with me just out of pity or just of convenience,

If you're not in love with me then let me go,

I don't need someone who's constantly breaking my heart,

I give you all the love I can and you repay me like this,

I'd understand if I'd abuse you or hurt you but I don't,

So tell me why are you still with me?

Is it for the love making?

If so you have got to go and let me find someone who'll appreciate me for all I have to offer.

My Journey

My journey is a dark one,

As I walk all I hear is agony and the cries of those I have hurt in the past,

Feeling all the pain and suffering around me,

Still searching for the light at the end of my tunnel,

But to no avail,…

I can't find this happiness people speak of,

As I go forth feeling heartbroken and alone,

My skin being ripped from my body,

Being tormented by all the negativity and despair surrounding me,

The darkness seems endless,

Just when I get a glimpse of light it moves further away,

Why must I be teased with a possibility when it seems so hard to obtain,

What must I do to end this realistic nightmare,

Hoping for love but I know I'm not worthy of it,

I continue on,

My will shattering with every step I take,

I sense hands trying to bring me down, but, I am not giving up,

The darkness keeps getting darker and I'm not sure how to get out,

Just need the most powerful and pure energy to get me through this,

Something called love.

No One

I have no one to love, hold, and to kiss,

No one to cuddle with, void in my heart grows,

No one to share my love with,

Wondering if love will ever find me,

No one to share my feelings n show how much I care,

My loneliness slowing consuming,

Should I try to find love even if it might break my heart again,

Feels like true love is a myth,

So why should I chase and search for it,

Alone again and hopefully I'll be able to be happy and get a final chance at love,

And I'll make sure I do it right this time,

For true love comes once in a lifetime and I was fortunate enough to have

had it more than that,

Should I deserve another chance… no,

But I hope I can be blessed for one last shot at it with whoever God sees fit for me.

Pain

My heart is shattered in a million pieces,

Should I give up on love,

Should I fight for the love,

I have failed her before,

Why should she give me another shot,

Maybe I deserve all these things that are happening to me,

Perhaps I'm meant to live miserable without love,

I lost my only chance for a happy family,

Think I should just accept that I failed her again and maybe she'll be happier

without me,

I'm probably no good to her as a friend due to muy feelings,

But my feelings don't matter anymore,

I'm worthless anyhow,

I will accept my fate and wait for the rest of the messed up stuff in my life to

attack me head on.

Spanish

Amor

Que es el amor,
Defrutando la vida con el amor tuyo,
Esperando los besos que me haces deretir,
Soñando de los momentos mas sensual,
Deseando los abrasos que te haces sentil protejida,
Recordandote las noches que tuvimos en passion,
Discuvriendo las areas que te haces temblar,
Y saviendo que junto con el amor nada faltara.

Dirme

Dirme que me amas como yo te amo,
Enseñame cuanto me amas si el amor tuyo es sinsero,
Escucha mi corazon y como tu me haces falta,
Quida mi corazon porque el es bien frajil,
Recuerdate de la primera vez que no vimos,
Y de nuestro primer beso,
Nunca te orvides,
Sin ti yo no podra ser complete.

Porque

Dirme porque no me amas,

Que e hecho para que te sientas asi,

Yo etratado lo maximo para complaserte,

Que a pasado,

Encontraste a otro?

Por favor dirme que puedo hacer para cambiar tu decision,

Si tengo que mover una montaña para quedarnos junto dirme qual es,

Mi corazón no podrás continual sin ti,

Arrodillado te pregunto dirme porque,

Tu me dises que te vas y no a dicho la razon,

Vete entonce,

Yo se que quando Dios quiera el me va a mandar una para mi que me ames para siempre.

Tu

Tu sonrisa illumina los dias,

Tu amor me compaña en las noches,

En tus ojos veo todo el cariño y compasión que tienes en tu corazón,

Los lavios tan tibio siempre preparada para besar,

Tu cuerpo para calentarme en el frio,

El amor que me as dado nadie mas pordra,

Y mi corazón es tuyo asta la muerte.

Religious

Love from Above

Have no fears,
Believe in Christ and he'll wipe away all your tears,
His love for us is more powerful than anything ever known,
Who else would forgive us no matter how bad we've been,
No one but Him,
Who died on the cross for our sins so we could go to heaven,
Christ that's who,
Who rose
from the dead proving that he's the son of God,
That's right Jesus Christ,
Believe that he died for us and rose up to save us from the eternal flame,
Then and only then are we truly saved from eternal damnation.

Religion

There are many kinas of religions in the world,
Ones that teach the word of God as it should be,
Others that use the word for their own purposes,
When searching for a temple of worship look for the one that teaches
about the Bible as God intended,
Don't go for the one that fits your style,
The church isn't suppose to conform around you,
You're suppose to conform to the word of God and the rules set by the Alpha and Omega,
We all have a purpose on the planet,
Your church (with God's leadership) will assist you in finding what that purpose is,
If you want the answer directly just ask and the lord will answer at his own discretion,
Be patient,
And be ready to listen because when He speaks you won't want to miss
what's in store.

Rain

Why does it rain when I'm crying,

Why does it rain when I'm depressed making me feel worst,

Why does it rain when I feel all alone in the world and no one

understands me,

When all my hopes and dreams are shattered it rains even harder,

When all the plans I made in advance & I'm in a great mood it still rains

messing up my day,

Why,

Then I realized,

When I was crying, depressed, and things weren't going well it would

rain,

Because I wasn't alone when all this was going on,

God's crying when I was at my worst & he's letting me know better days

are on their way,

When I was doing fine and it would rain,

He was comforting someone who needed his love.

Stressed

Life is full of second chances,

I hope and pray that I learn to utilize it and not mess it up like the other times,

Disappointing everyone that ever trusted me,

Hopefully I get another chance,

Because my opportunities are almost all used up,

With a tear in my eye and a heavy heart,

I look up at the night sky painted a bluish black accompanied by the stars which seems endless,

I begin to pray,

Lord,

Please guide me,

Jesus, please forgive me for all the people I hurt physically, mentally, and emotionally,

Forgive me for all those souls I have corrupted,

Forgive me for all the lies, deception, infidelity,

If it is your will,

Please show my wife that I sincerely am remorsed for the wrongs I've done,

For the heartache and pain accompanied by stress with all trust lost for me,

Lord,

I know I am not worthy of her love and affection,

Please show me or teach me how to deal with my daughter's illness,

I don't know how to raise her and help my wife with her,

All the events that happened was all my fault,

Lord,

Maybe this is a nightmare,

If it is then I'll end my life so I can wake up,

What if it's not,

Then there'll be no way of knowing if my life ends up staying with my wife and me making her happy and trusting me again,

Jesus,

I know I'm not worthy of a second chance but I hope you grant me one,

Guide me on changing,

Show me and teach me how I can be or what I can do in order to receive that wonderful, incredible, blessed second chance to make things right,

Amen.

Thank you for listening; I am wits end,

Please hear my cries,

She's the only one I can picture growing old with.

Am I Not Your Child

When I was going through rough times; where were you?
When I was crying and feeling depressed; you weren't around,
When I was constantly tempted; you didn't try to stop me,
Also when my mother almost died from asthma; I prayed,
Through it all I prayed; you never answered,
If I am truly your child then why did I go through it alone?
Then…
At that precise moment; I heard Him in all his Glory,
A deep, warm, caring, peaceful voice say;
Of course you are my child,
When you were in troubled times; who do you think sent you people
dealing with the same issues,
While you were crying and depressed; who do you think sent you
brothers from church to keep you company,
During your temptations; I knew you would make me proud,
When your mother was ill; it was your prayer that helped her,
I was by your side the entire time,
I heard all your prayers,
I sent you signs to let you know of my presence,
The reason you didn't see it,
You were too busy worrying about everything else instead of putting all
your faith in me.

Depressed

Pain, frustrated, hopeless,

Too many feelings to express,

So many situations to handle and no way to deal with them,

Due to an injury I can't provide much financially,

Feeling useless,

Not being able to play the role as the "provider",

Tired of stressing over my physical pain,

Having to deal with myself made mental torture,

Mostly thinking I must deal with all the conflicts alone,

Why should I burden anyone else when it's my problem to deal with,

I pray and pray but I guess it's not my time to be heard,

Everyone says everything will get better,

But how do they know if they've never been where I'm at right now,

Lord; I pray once again,

Please hear my plea; if not for me then for my family,

Take care of them in the times when I can not,

May it be financially, physically, or spiritually,

Until I can,

For you are the only one who can help them where as I am helpless,

Grant me the strength to recover faster,

In order to handle my duties and erase this horrible feeling of depression.

Amen.

Upcoming Poets

Every Night

Every night I look up at the stars hoping you see them too,

Now all I do is cry knowing I'm alone in my emotions,

All I wanted was to show you my love; to hold and kiss even one day I

hoped to call you my wife,

But I know now that was just a dream; and I feel the sharp knife,

Stabbing into my heart; I cry myself to sleep because my heart still calls

for you,

But I know now I'm the wolf who loves the moon; I cry like the wolf howls

at a love that I can't have,

That's the sad truth I must live with... God

please help me.

By: Michael Ortiz

When

What is happiness?
I know it exists,
Because everyone around me is at their happiest,
But why can't I find it,
Where did it go,
Is it hiding; I really don't know,
Why all I can find is depression and sadness,
When will I ever be able to find,
Something called happiness.

By Natalia Figueroa

Prophet

Truth is treason; in an empire of lies,
And nobodies winning; when everyone dies,
So I ask the simple questions; in an obvious way,
And slowly all the people; listen to what I say,
Ill and I'll learn; and devote my time,
Until I completely; lose my mind,
I jumped down a rabbit hole; I fell quite a spell,
And now I'm seeing visions; of things they won't tell,
So when logic has failed me; and words can't describe,
I'll dig deeper down; and put god on my side,
I'll lead by example; and the people will follow,
A wounded phoenix; that the system made hollow,
And the very moment; that people rally,
We'll stop the wars; we'll erase the tally,
This is how; a prophet is made,
By the people who chose him; and the lives that he saved,
And if the prophet; dies in war,
He becomes a martyr; forever more,
But the idea won't die; it stays alive,
In people like me; who refuse to comply,
Refuse to accept this; refuse the oppression,
And if I don't make it; this is my confession,
I've accepted my fate; I embrace it completely,
And I'll die for the cause; so that you can live freely.

By: Nikki Zukoski

Acknowledgments

I would like to thank all the artists and poets that contributed to this project. Without them, my dream would've never become a reality. Next, I thank the people who believed in me, when I didn't believe in myself. Finally, I would like to thank the publishing company for helping me make all this happen for everyone to see.

If you enjoyed any of the artworks or poems, here are the names of the artist and poets. You can contact them to critic or compliment their work; also, for additional information on future projects or collaborations.

Michael Ortiz   Beastking1292@gmail.com
Nikki Zukoski   Nikkisixx1588@gmail.com

Printed in the United States
By Bookmasters